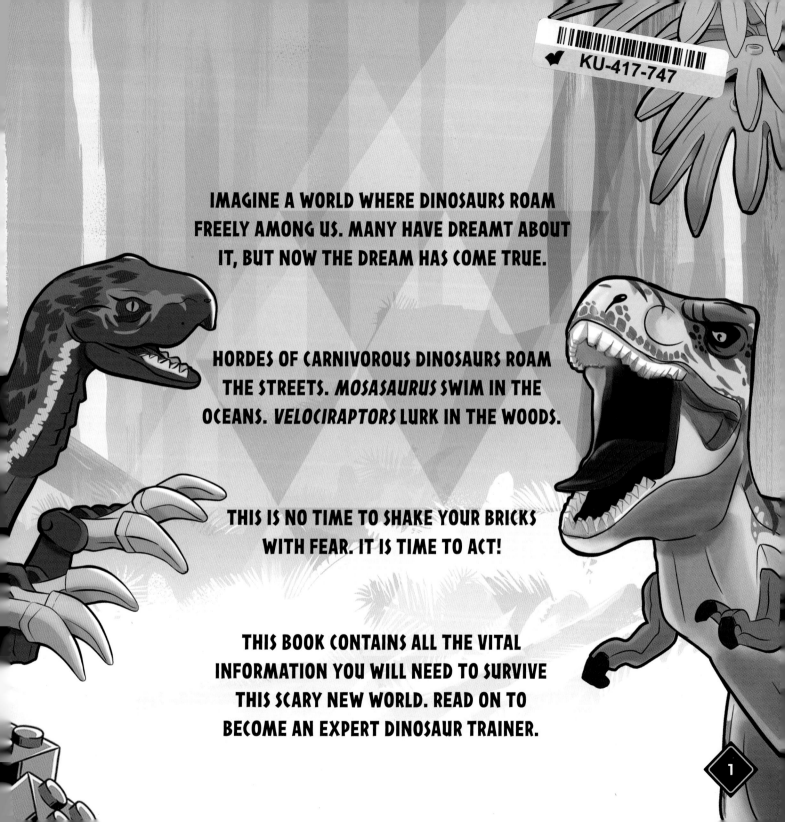

IMAGINE A WORLD WHERE DINOSAURS ROAM FREELY AMONG US. MANY HAVE DREAMT ABOUT IT, BUT NOW THE DREAM HAS COME TRUE.

HORDES OF CARNIVOROUS DINOSAURS ROAM THE STREETS. *MOSASAURUS* SWIM IN THE OCEANS. *VELOCIRAPTORS* LURK IN THE WOODS.

THIS IS NO TIME TO SHAKE YOUR BRICKS WITH FEAR. IT IS TIME TO ACT!

THIS BOOK CONTAINS ALL THE VITAL INFORMATION YOU WILL NEED TO SURVIVE THIS SCARY NEW WORLD. READ ON TO BECOME AN EXPERT DINOSAUR TRAINER.

ATROCIRAPTOR

(AT-ROH-SEE-RAP-TOR)

Carnivore

Aggression
Intelligence

CHARACTERISTICS

This dinosaur has been modified to be even larger, faster and more dangerous than other raptors. Infamous individuals such as Ghost, Panthera, Red and Tiger will attack without hesitation when ordered to do so.

HABITS

The *Atrociraptor* hunts in a pack, and is always hungry. He can eat a ton of food and come back for seconds.

GOOD ADVICE

- Steer well clear!

- If you come across an *Atrociraptor*, a *T. rex* can provide a distraction. Then again, that might just be double trouble.

- If there's no *T. rex* around, just give him all of your food (and you had better have a lot of it) and then run!

DILOPHOSAURUS

(DIE-LO-PHO-SAW-RUS)

Carnivore

Aggression
Intelligence

CHARACTERISTICS

The *Dilophosaurus* will open up the crest on her neck like a fan, to make her opponent (or dinner) freeze in fear. When that doesn't work, she can use her venom.

HABITS

This dinosaur loves peas and broccoli ... NOT! She is one hungry carnivore, and she's hungry for meat of any kind. When *Dilophosaurus* is angry or thinks someone looks tasty, she raises her crest and lets out a startling hiss.

GOOD ADVICE

- Always carry a mirror. When a *Dilophosaurus* sees a mirror, she gets distracted and spits venom at her own reflection.
- Never feed a *Dilophosaurus*. She will want you for dessert!
- If you open two big fans at a *Dilophosaurus*, she will think you're opening your crest and run away. Those fans could be your only hope.

GIGANOTOSAURUS

(GIG-AN-OH-TOE-SAW-RUS)

Carnivore

Aggression
Intelligence

HABITS

Giganotosaurus is bigger and more dangerous than a *T. rex*. He can eat a full truck of chicken drumsticks – including the truck! He lives alone, because he can't stand to share his food.

CHARACTERISTICS

The *Giganotosaurus* is the king of Biosyn Valley. His massive size, huge jaws and warpaint-like skin are enough to terrify anyone unlucky enough to get in his way.

GOOD ADVICE

- If you hear him coming, there's just one thing you need to do: RUN!

- A truck of chicken drumsticks might be just enough to keep a *Giganotosaurus* busy while you make your escape.

- If you don't have a truck of chicken drumsticks, it's time to get one!

MOSASAURUS

(MO-SA-SAW-RUS)

Carnivore

Aggression

Intelligence

CHARACTERISTICS

This water giant is the ruler of the oceans. Her massive teeth and powerful body are her greatest weapons. It's no surprise to learn that some call the *Mosasaurus* "the *T. rex* of the sea".

HABITS

Mosasaurus is the most dangerous swimmer around, and preys on the biggest fish she can find. Although she spends most of her time underwater, she must come up to the surface to breathe.

GOOD ADVICE

- Don't go swimming where a *Mosasaurus* lives, or you'll probably become breakfast.
- Don't take a kayak or boat to a *Mosasaurus*' home either. You'll still be breakfast, but served on a floating plate.
- You're not even safe when taking a walk along the beach with an ice cream. A *Mosasaurus* could burst out of the water and snatch the ice cream from you!

TRICERATOPS

(TRY-SER-A-TOPS)

Herbivore

Aggression

Intelligence

HABITS

The *Triceratops* loves peace, quiet and large green areas where she can eat in peace. However, don't be fooled. When disturbed, *Triceratops* behaves like a battering ram.

CHARACTERISTICS

What the *Triceratops* lacks in intelligence she makes up for in strength. Those massive horns can pose a serious threat to even a *T. rex*. *Triceratops* will do whatever it takes to protect herself and her herd.

GOOD ADVICE

- Never eat a carrot near a *Triceratops*. This giant will run through a wall for the chance to munch on some vegetables.

- Once a *Triceratops* is quietly eating, you can try to pat her – but only with the permission of a Biosyn Genetics employee.

- If a *Triceratops* runs towards you, make sure you climb a tree or even step to one side. Just don't stand still.

PTERANODON

(TERR-AN-OH-DON)

Carnivore

Aggression
Intelligence

CHARACTERISTICS

Pteranodons live in flocks, just like birds. They love to eat fish (just as long as the fish isn't big enough to eat them) and they love to play.

HABITS

A *Pteranodon* will eat any kind of fish: fried, baked, raw, even canned! They build their nests up high, and swoop down whenever they spot a chance for a meal.

GOOD ADVICE

- Never sit in a *Pteranodon's* nest. They really don't like that.

- If you see a *Pteranodon* circling over your head, find an old pot and bang it to make lots of noise. The *Pteranodon* will soon move on.

- If a flock of *Pteranodons* dives towards you, throw them a ball. While they're busy playing with the ball, you can make a run for it.

PYRORAPTOR

(PY-RO-RAP-TOR)

Carnivore

Aggression

Intelligence

CHARACTERISTICS

The *Pyroraptor* is as clever and aggressive as a *Velociraptor*, but prefers to hunt alone. *Pyroraptor's* feathers offer protection in both jungle thickets and snowy mountains.

HABITS

Don't be fooled by the fluffy feathers and colourful crest. The *Pyroraptor* is a dangerous carnivore who could gobble down cartloads of hot dogs and still see you as a snack.

GOOD ADVICE

- Forget about trying to take any of those feathers as a souvenir.

- Don't try to feed birdseed to this fine feathered creature. A *Pyroraptor* will ignore the seed and come for you instead!

- *Pyroraptor* may look like a bird, but he can't fly – so, if he spots you, climb a tree.

QUETZALCOATLUS

(KWET-ZAL-CO-AT-LUS)

 Omnivore

Aggression
Intelligence

HABITS

The *Quetzalcoatlus* can travel great distances through the air. Those enormous wings allow her to easily fly from continent to continent.

CHARACTERISTICS

Quetzalcoatlus doesn't need to fear any other dinosaurs. If anything, it's the other dinosaurs who should be scared. *Quetzalcoatlus* likes to chase aeroplanes and sometimes even snatches cars from the ground.

GOOD ADVICE

- A *Quetzalcoatlus* is a threat even when not flying. She can move around surprisingly quickly on her legs.

- If you see a *Quetzalcoatlus* while in a plane, change course immediately. You'll be seen as a rival, and likely come off second best.

- The *Quetzalcoatlus* loves to swoop down on speeding cars just for fun. If you see one above your car, take cover under trees as soon as you can.

THERIZINOSAURUS

(THER-IH-ZEEN-OH-SAW-RUS)

Herbivore

Aggression
Intelligence

18

HABITS

The *Therizinosaurus* prefers plants to meat, so there's no need to be afraid. Unless you happen to step on her tail, that is!

CHARACTERISTICS

The *Therizinosaurus* is a gentle dinosaur whose large claws are used only for gathering food from the trees. However, she still knows how to defend herself and will even stand up to a *Giganotosaurus*.

GOOD ADVICE

- Don't step on her tail, and you'll have no problems.
- If you spot a *Therizinosaurus* eating fruit from a tree, find a different fruit tree for yourself.
- If you see a *Therizinosaurus* fighting a *Giganotosaurus*, make a run for it. Unless you have a truck full of chicken drumsticks for the *Giganotosaurus*, that is.

TYRANNOSAURUS REX

(TIE-RAN-OH-SAW-RUS REX)

Carnivore

Aggression

Intelligence

HABITS

This is a real dino-star! The *T. rex* strolls around proudly, making the ground tremble. If you have meat, the *T. rex* will eat it – and she will probably try to eat you, too.

CHARACTERISTICS

The mighty *T. rex* will never shy away from a fight or a chase. No matter the situation, this enormous carnivore is always ready to rumble.

GOOD ADVICE

- Keep an eye on the ground. When it starts to shake, it means a *T. rex* is coming.

- If you need to distract a *T. rex*, throw a flare as far as you can – or light up the Christmas tree! *T. rex* loves lights.

- Hiding in a car won't save you. A *T. rex* will bite straight through it. You'd be better off looking for a tank instead.

VELOCIRAPTOR

(VEL-OSS-IH-RAP-TOR)

Carnivore

Aggression

Intelligence